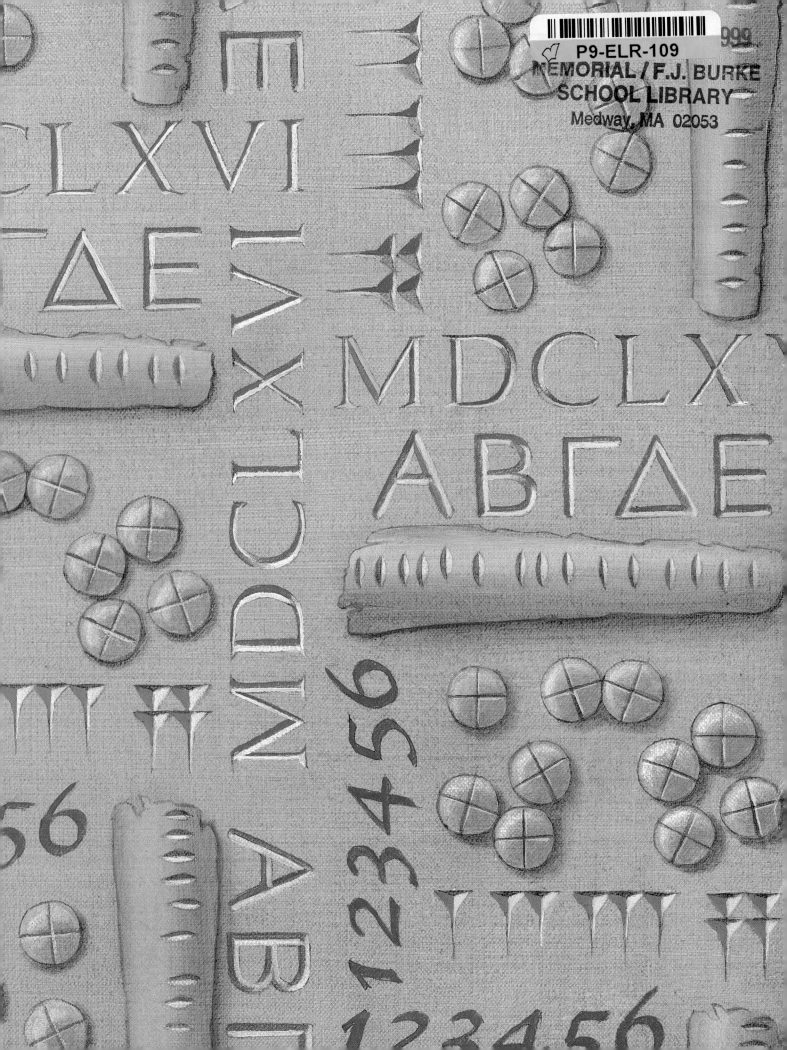

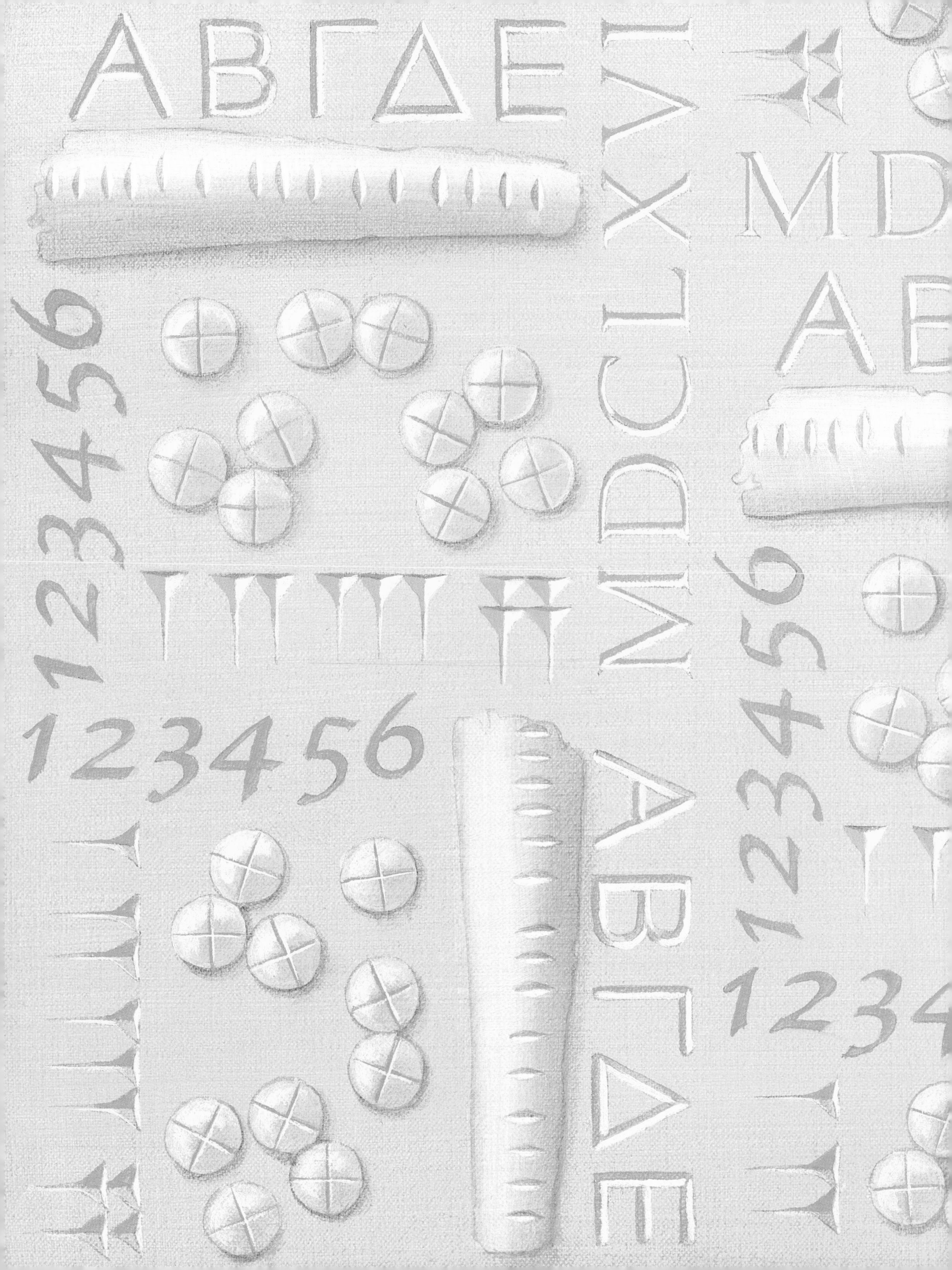

ΑΒΓΔΕ

123456

123456

1234 56

ΧΥΙ

ΜΟ

ΑΕ

ΜΟCL

ΜΟCM

ΑΒ

123456

123456

1234

ΑΒΓ

ΔΕ

THE
HISTORY
OF
COUNTING

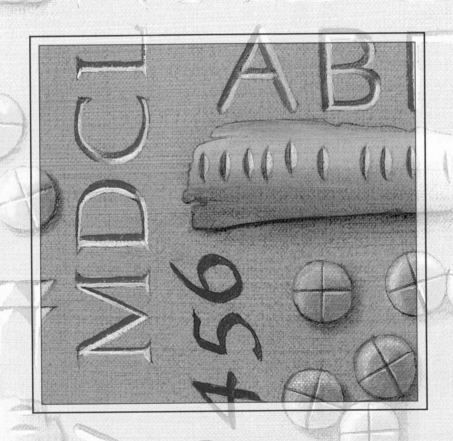

DENISE SCHMANDT-BESSERAT
ILLUSTRATED BY MICHAEL HAYS

MORROW JUNIOR BOOKS • NEW YORK

To Nicolaus with love
—D.S.B.

To David Macaulay, for pointing me
toward the unexplored possibilities of
the picture book
—M.H.

The help of Helen Conover, a partner in FUNdamental Science,
an elementary science education consulting firm in New York City,
is gratefully acknowledged.

Acrylic on linen was used for the full-color illustrations.
The text type is 13.5-point Garamond Book.

Published by Morrow Junior Books
a division of William Morrow and Company, Inc.
1350 Avenue of the Americas, New York, NY 10019

Printed in Hong Kong by South China Printing Company (1988) Ltd.

1 2 3 4 5 6 7 8 9 10

Library of Congress Cataloging-in-Publication Data
Schmandt-Besserat, Denise.
The history of counting/Denise Schmandt-Besserat; illustrated by Michael Hays.
p. cm.
Includes index.
Summary: Describes the evolution of counting and
the many ways to count and write numbers.
ISBN 0-688-14118-8 (trade)—ISBN 0-688-14119-6 (library)
1. Counting—History—Juvenile literature.   2. Numeration—Juvenile literature.
[1. Counting.   2. Number systems.]   I. Hays, Michael, ill.   II. Title.
QA113.S386 1999   513.5—dc20   96-35316   CIP AC

INTRODUCTION

A number is a word that expresses "how many."

Counting is reciting numbers in order. Counting the ducklings on the pond, for example, means reciting, "One, two, three, four, five...," as each duckling swims by. The last number tells how many ducklings are on the pond.

Surprising as it may seem, people did not always have numbers. For most of their time on earth, in fact, modern humans had no numbers. Imagine not having numbers. What would life be like without counting?

Today, numbers play an important role. We use them in many ways: They show the price of things; tell the hours of the day and the days of the months; mark the houses on the street; make it easy to find the right bus or dial the telephone; identify cars and tell the players of a team apart.

In this book you will discover how the numbers 0, 1, 2, 3, 4, 5, 6, 7, 8, 9—and the system of counting that uses them—were invented.

Today, people of most areas of the world—including North and South America, Europe, Asia, Africa, and Australia—share the same efficient counting system. With only these ten *digits*—0, 1, 2, 3, 4, 5, 6, 7, 8, 9—we can make up any number we want.

Our way of counting is not the only one, though. There are people in some parts of the globe who do not count the way we do. In the recent past, the Veddas of Sri Lanka, who lived by eating the fruit and tubers of jungle plants, had only a few general words, such as *a single, a couple, another one,* and *many,* to deal with numbers.

Because of their simple way of life, the Veddas got along just fine without numbers. When a Vedda wished to count coconuts, for instance, he collected pebbles. For each coconut he took a pebble: one coconut = one pebble. For each pebble he counted "another one." When he was finished, he pointed to his pile of pebbles and said, "That many." The way the Veddas counted is called *counting without numbers.* What is it good for? Whenever the Vedda wanted to, he could check if his pile of coconuts was complete just by comparing it with his pile of pebbles.

Other people never created special words for numbers. For example, the Paiela, who cultivate orchards in the highlands of Papua New Guinea, count by pointing to parts of their body. The number 1 is called "left little finger," 11 is "left neck," 16 is "right ear," etc. This way of counting is called *body counting*. When the Paiela go to the marketplace, they trade and bargain by pointing to their fingers, wrists, elbows, shoulders, neck, and nose. At the same time they say the word for that part of the body. This way of counting is sufficient in communities that have no use for large numbers, because the people themselves produce most of the food and things they need. (The largest number of the Paiela is 28, shown by the two hands clenched together.)

Body counting must have been quite widespread around the globe as late as the 1800s. It was also used, for instance, by native peoples of Paraguay, South America, whose largest number was 20, shown by pointing to the two feet.

When and why did people invent body counting? No one knows, because there is no record of how it came about and for what purpose. The past of people who, like the Paiela, have no writing may soon be forgotten. However, body counting tells us an important fact: The idea of using numbers as special symbols did not happen by chance. The fact that some peoples never created special words like *two* and *three* shows that numbers had to be invented.

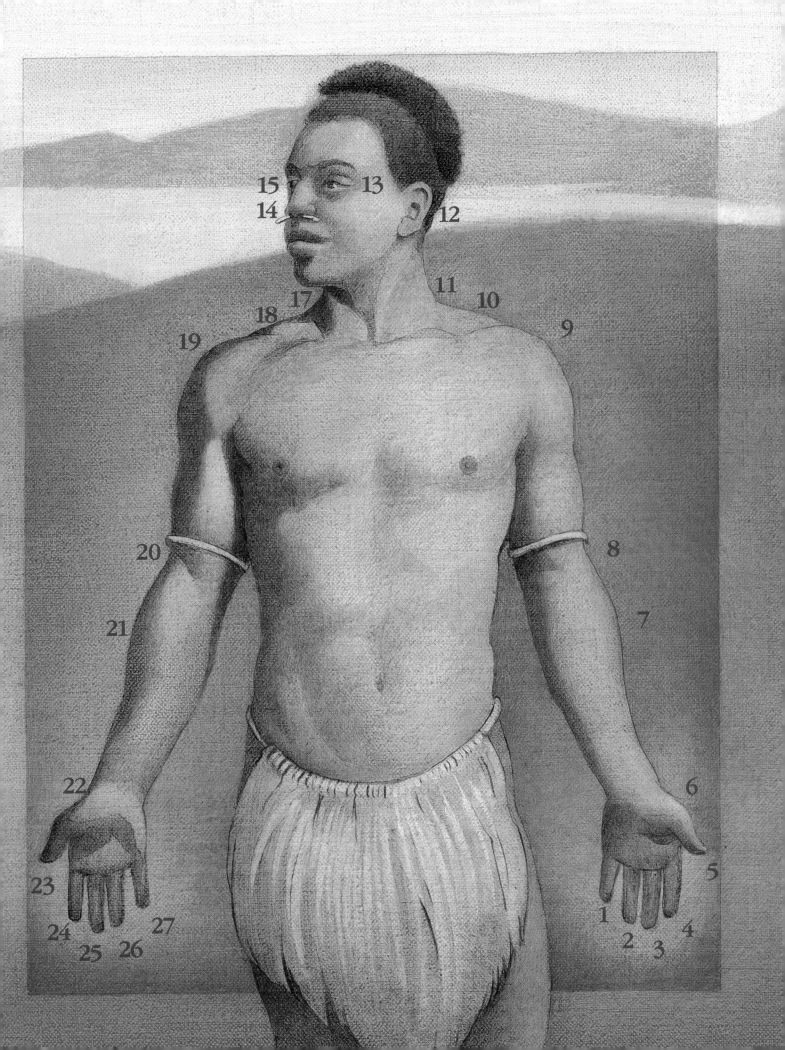

Still other peoples count *concretely*. This means that they use different *sets*, or groups, of numbers to count different categories of things.

For example, the Gilyaks, who farm along the river Amur, in eastern Russia, have twenty-four sets of numbers. When a Gilyak counts trees, sticks, pencils, and some other long things, she uses the word *mex* for the number 2. When counting leaves, pieces of textile, and other flat items, she will use *met* for 2. And for berries, balls, and other round things, 2 becomes *mik*.

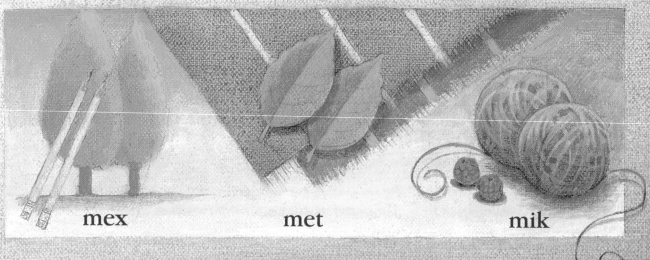

mex   met   mik

Note also that the Gilyaks' number sequences never reach much beyond 20. In other words, concrete numbers do not allow large quantities to be counted.

Concrete counting shows how societies around the world faced the problem of handling *plurality*, or groups of many items, and found different solutions to express numbers.

The concrete numbers are similar to our terms *twins, triplets, quadruplets*, which refer to the number of children of the same birth, and *duo, trio, quartet*, which refer to groups of musicians. Both number words—*twins* and *duo*—indicate 2. But in neither case does the word separate the *number* from the *thing* that is being counted.

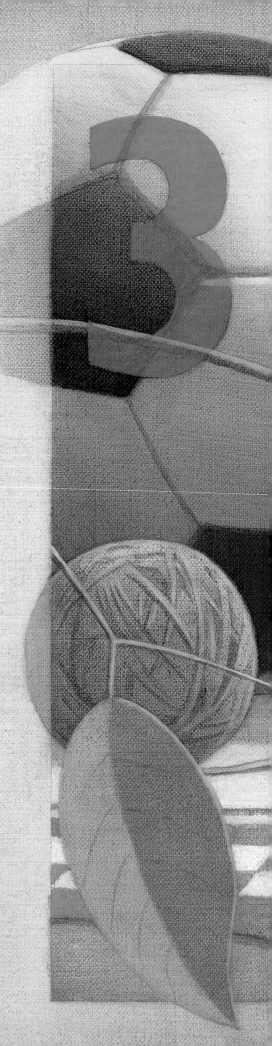

The most universal way of counting, the one the majority of people use today, is known as *abstract counting,* using abstract numbers. We separate, or abstract, the *idea* of "one," "two," "three," and so on, from the *thing* we are counting. This system is very convenient because:

- Abstract numbers count anything.
- Each abstract number is expressed by a word that remains the same no matter what is being counted.

   (This is not so with concrete counting. In that system, number words are limited to counting small amounts of only certain types of common things of daily life.)

Another advantage is that abstract numbers are infinite. For example, our largest numbers are the googol (a 1 followed by one hundred zeros) and the googolplex (a 1 followed by a googol of zeros). But if we ever needed to count beyond these numbers, we could keep adding zeros like this:
10000000000000000000000000000000000000000
00000000000000000000000000000000000000000
00000000000000000000000000000000000000000
00000000000000000000000000000000000000000
00000000000000000000000000000000000000000
00000000000000000000000000000000000000000
00000000000000000000000000000000000000000
00000000000000000000000000000000000000000
00000000000000000000000000000000000000…

14

three

Mathematicians think that abstract counting developed over a long period of time. Some suggest that the evolution of counting may have happened in three steps: *1.* counting without numbers, *2.* concrete counting, and *3.* abstract counting. Ancient objects used for counting found in the Middle East support this idea.

The earliest counting devices are notched bones that were found among the remains of hunters and gatherers who lived about fifteen thousand years ago in what is now the Middle East. Although we do not know *what* these ancient people counted with the notched bones, these counting devices may tell *how* they counted. Because each notch is similar to the next one and because there never seems to be a total indicated on the bones, it is likely that the hunters and gatherers had not yet developed numbers. Each notch probably stood for "and one more."

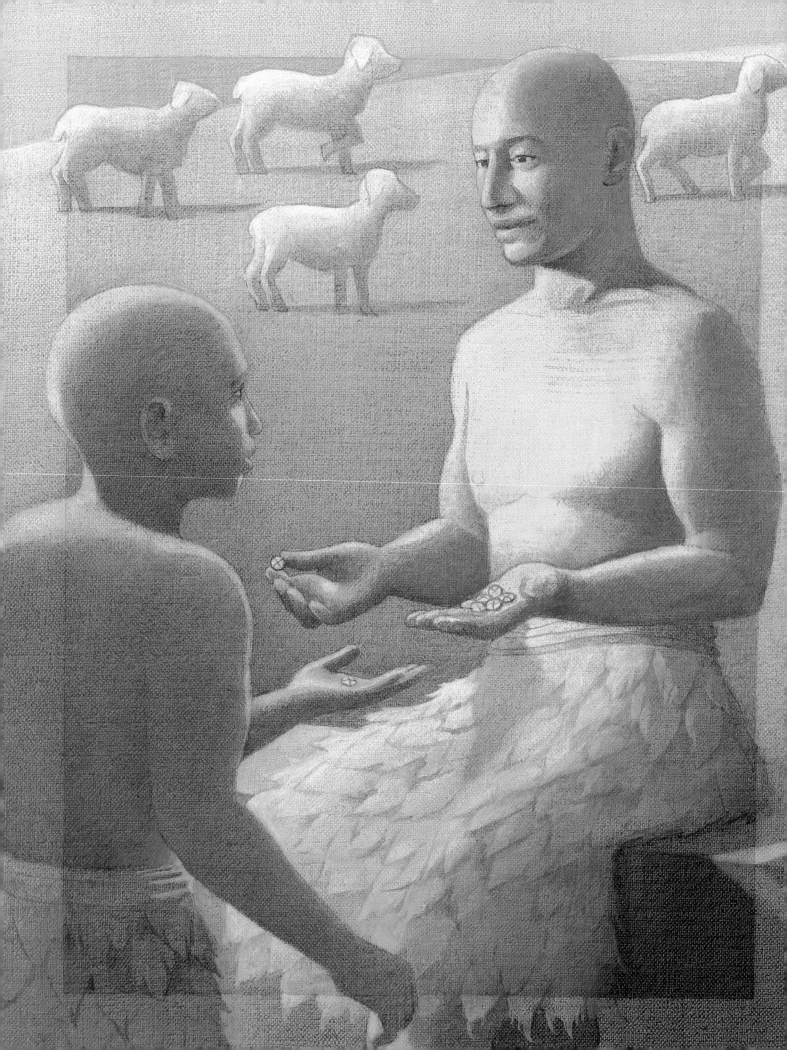

The counters found in the villages and towns built by farmers between five thousand and ten thousand years ago were small tokens of many shapes. Each token shape was used to count only one type of thing. For example, sheep were counted with disks, but jars of oil were counted with egg-shaped tokens. (We know this because the signs for *sheep* and *oil* in early Sumerian writing pictured a disk and an egg shape.)

The fact that each different type of item was counted with a different-shaped token suggests that the early farmers had different sets of numbers to count various things. They counted concretely. They used the tokens by matching them with the number of things counted: One sheep was shown by one disk, two sheep by two disks, and so on.

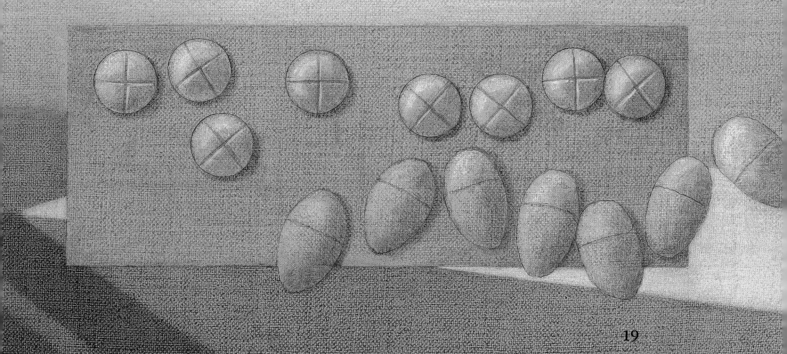

We owe the invention of abstract numbers to the Sumerians who lived in the first cities, in the region of present-day Iraq, about five thousand years ago. The Sumerian tablet in the man's hand shows an account of thirty-three jars of oil. The sign on the right stands for "jar of oil." The other signs represent numbers. Each circle is 10, and each long sign is 1. (For more on the Sumerian counting system, see page 24.)

Why is this counting system different from the others? For the first time, number and things counted were separated, or abstracted. Sheep and jars of oil were finally counted with the same numbers!

Why did it take thousands and thousands of years to invent abstract numbers? Why weren't they invented sooner? It was not a question of intelligence: The size of your brain is the same as that of a child who lived fifty thousand years ago. Probably it was a matter of need. The simple life of hunters and gatherers required little counting, since these people lived on the animals they caught or the plants and fruits they gathered daily. The fact that it was the first farmers who invented tokens suggests that domesticating animals and plants made counting necessary. It makes a lot of sense that counting became important when the life of a community depended on knowing how many bags of grain to keep for planting the next harvest and how many animals would feed the village during the winter season.

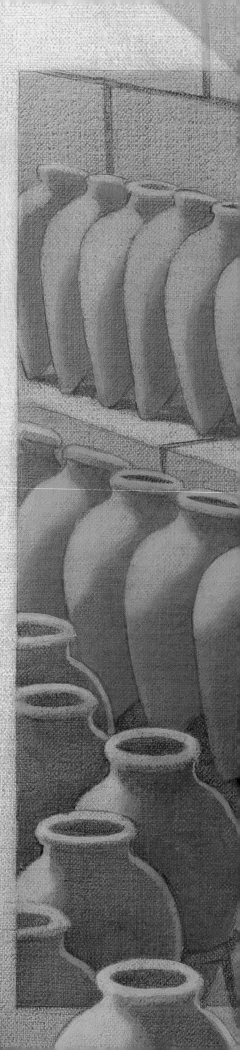

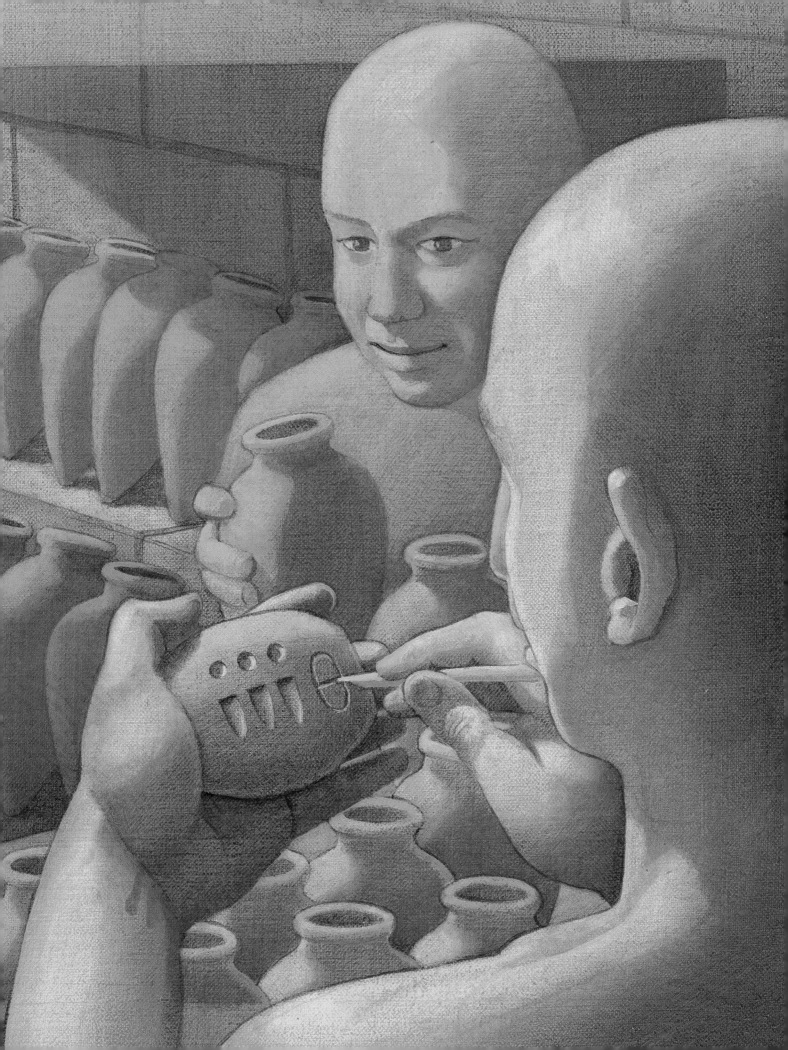

There can also be no doubt that abstract counting was invented to cope with the development of business, trade, and taxes in the first cities. A more precise method of counting became necessary once workshops produced quantities of pottery and tools. But it was the tax system that had the biggest impact on counting. Every month, each Sumerian had to deliver to the ruler specific amounts of fish, oil, grain, or animals. Because of this, the palace accountants had to come up with a way to keep track of large amounts of goods.

The three steps in counting, therefore, were responses to new demands brought about by the increased complexity of life.

Once abstract numbers were invented, they were used more and more widely in trade and in calculations needed for everyday life.

And with the greater use of numbers also came the need for larger and larger numbers. In the country of Sumer, the most common large number that was used in everyday life was 60. It was called "the big one," which suggests that, at some time, it had been the highest number. But by 2500 B.C., the Sumerians' largest number had grown to 36,000. It was probably used very rarely and then only by palace accountants to calculate tax collections.

It is much the same for our large numbers today. The googol and the googolplex were invented in the 1950s by mathematicians who needed to do very large calculations. But we never use these large numbers in daily life. The largest numbers we read about in newspapers are in the trillions. One trillion is a 1 followed by twelve zeros.

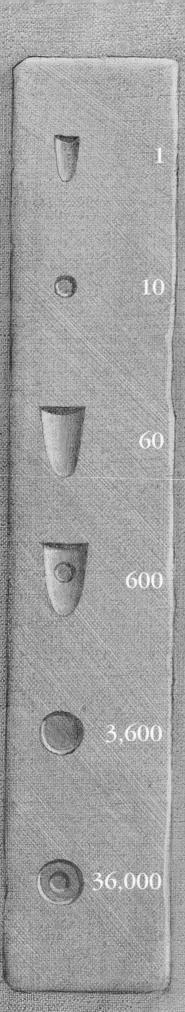

1

10

60

600

3,600

36,000

Signs to represent numbers are called *numerals*. The Sumerians had distinct signs to represent 1, 10, 60, 600, 3,600, and 36,000. The remaining numbers were shown by repeating these signs. For instance, the sign for 1 was a long wedge, and the numbers 2 through 9 were shown by two to nine wedges. The number 10 was a circular sign, and 20 through 50 were shown by two to five circular signs. The number 60 was a large wedge.

In Sumer, reading a numeral like 23 meant counting how many circles or wedges were included in the numeral.

The numbers 10 and 60 were special in Sumer, because they were bases. *Bases* are numbers used to create higher numbers. The Sumerian large numbers were multiplications of these numbers:

$$10 \times 60 = 600$$
$$60 \times 60 = 3,600$$
$$60 \times 60 \times 10 = 36,000$$

Why did the Sumerians give such importance to 60? Because this number has a unique advantage: It can be divided equally in many ways. The number 60 is divisible by 1, 2, 3, 4, 5, 6, 10, 12, 15, 20, 30, and 60. This is why we have hours of 60 minutes and minutes of 60 seconds. If one hour was divided into ten minutes, it could be divided equally in only four ways: by 1, 2, 5, and 10.

The system of counting we use today has one base: 10. In this system—called *decimal,* after the Latin word for "ten"—large numbers are multiplications of 10. For example, 10 x 10 = 100, and 10 x 10 x 10 = 1,000.

While the Sumerians' system of counting was remarkable for their time, it did have a drawback: It had no zero. In other words, the Sumerians had no sign to indicate "no value." They just left a space.

This was unclear and led to difficulties in reading numbers. You can see this for yourself. Look at the number 204,501. How easy is it to read without the zeros—2 4,5 1?

Although the shape of the numerals changed, the Sumerians' counting system itself was used for centuries. The Babylonians were still using it two thousand years later, around 600 B.C.

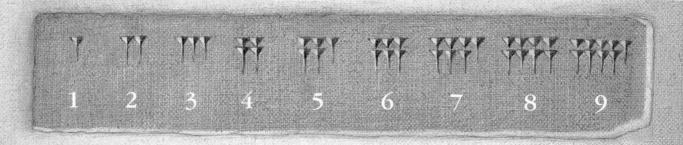

Why was such a complicated counting system used for so long? Perhaps because it is easier to follow old ways of thinking than to come up with new ways and innovate.

The Phoenicians, who invented the alphabet around 1500 B.C., innovated. They used the letters of their alphabet as numerals and had only base 10.

The Phoenicians' innovations show that counting evolved by leaps and bounds. Although we would like to know why, where, and when the alphabet was invented and how the letters became used as numerals, the memory of such events is lost.

GREEK

A	B	Γ	Δ	E	Ϲ	Z	H	Θ	I	K	Λ	M	N
1	2	3	4	5	6	7	8	9	10	20	30	40	50

We do know that by 500 B.C., the Greeks had borrowed the Phoenician system. They used twenty-seven letters of their alphabet as numerals. The first nine letters were the digits 1 through 9. The next nine letters were the tens, and the last nine letters were the hundreds. The last letter stood for 900.

The Greek numeral system shows that the people of Athens seldom dealt with more than hundreds in daily life. However, Greek state accountants and mathematicians had a system of writing numerals beyond 900. 1,000 to 9,000 was shown by the sign ' to the upper left of the number. For example:

$$\text{'A} = 1,000$$

10,000 to 190,000 was indicated by placing an **M** (the Greek letter mu) below the numeral. For example:

$$\overset{\epsilon}{\text{M}} = 50,000$$

The Greek numeral system was troublesome, because it used as many as twenty-seven signs. By 200 B.C., the Romans improved on it by reducing the number of signs to seven letters.

Once again, the fact that the common numerals did not reach

ROMAN

I	V	X	L
1	5	10	50

Ξ	Ο	Π	Ϛ	Ρ	Σ	Τ	Υ	Φ	Χ	Ψ	Ω	ϻ
60	70	80	90	100	200	300	400	500	600	700	800	900

beyond 1,000 indicates how infrequently large numbers were used in everyday life in Rome. But here too, state accountants and mathematicians had a system of expressing higher numbers. They added a line over the numeral:

$$\overline{V} = 5,000 \qquad \overline{X} = 10,000$$

The Phoenicians, Greeks, and Romans had a limited set of numerals—the highest numeral in the Greek system was 900, and for the Romans, it was 1,000. When they needed to count above that, they had to use complex systems of markings. And, following the Phoenicians, the Greeks and the Romans used the base 10—but, still, neither of them had zero.

The Romans' numeral system depended on *place value.* This means that the number takes a different value according to its place. In the Romans' system, when a smaller number *follows* a larger one, the two numbers are combined, or *added,* together. For instance, XI equals 11. But when a smaller number *precedes* a larger number, the smaller number is *subtracted,* or taken away, from the larger number, so IX equals 9.

Place value reduced the number of special signs to remember. However, reading Roman numerals still meant adding or subtracting how many ones, fives, tens, and so on, were included in the numeral.

C	D	M
100	500	1,000

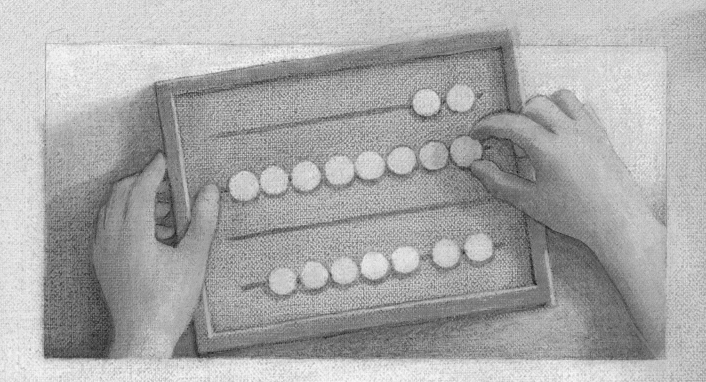

In Rome, these numerals were used for recording totals, but the actual computing was done with counters on a counting board that had horizontal lines drawn on it.

Counting started with the largest units. Each thousand was matched to a counter that was placed on the top line of the counting board, the line standing for 1,000. Then the hundreds were matched to counters that were placed on the line below, followed by the tens and the units. All the counters were computed together, and the result was recorded with numerals. For example, two thousand (MM) eight hundred (DCCC) and seven (VII) was written MMDCCCVII.

Roman numerals were still commonly used when Christopher Columbus set sail in 1492. And we still use them occasionally—for showing dates on buildings, for numbering volumes and chapters in books, and when indicating the hours on some clocks.

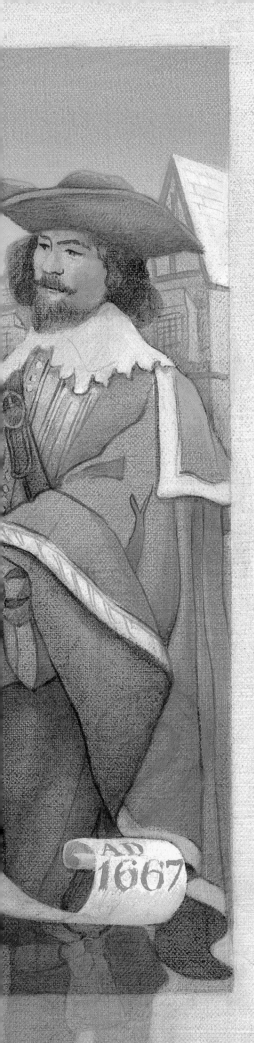

But when we add, subtract, multiply, and divide, we use digits called Arabic numerals. And we write them as 0 1 2 3 4 5 6 7 8 9.

Where and when the Arabic numerals were invented is a mystery. So is the identity of their inventor. Why then are the digits of our counting system called Arabic numerals? Because it was the Arabs who brought them to Europe, around the year A.D. 1000, when they ruled Spain. The Arabs, however, called these digits Hindu numerals, because they had borrowed them from India. The earliest document bearing such numerals was written in the ancient Indian Sanskrit language, about fifteen hundred years ago. No one knows how long the system was used before that or what preceded it.

The transition from Roman to Arabic numerals took centuries. The Europeans refused to change the old ways, saying, for instance, that the signs for 2 and 3 could be easily confused. Finally, by around 1650, Arabic numerals were fully accepted in Europe, and they still make up the number system used today.

Arabic numerals make counting and computing far easier than any previous systems. Why?

The first advantage has to do with the numerals used.

- There are separate symbols for each of the ten digits. This means, for example, 3 was no longer the repeated unit I (III), 4 was no longer 5 with a subtracted unit (IV), 6 was no longer 5 with an added unit (VI), and so on.
- The ten digits 0 to 9 can be used to create numbers indefinitely. On the other hand, the twenty-seven Greek letters reached only to 900, and the seven Roman numerals to 1,000. If people needed to count higher, new signs had to be invented.

0	1	2	3	4
zero	one	two	three	four

The second advantage is that the names for the numbers are repeated, and so are easy to memorize:

- Each digit, 0 to 9, has an individual name—0 is zero, 1 is one, 2 is two, continuing through 9 is nine. So do multiplications of 10 by 10—10 x 10 is hundred, 10 x 10 x 10 is thousand, and so on.
- The names of all other numbers are combinations (with the exception of eleven and twelve in English). For example: twenty; twenty-one; two hundred and one; two thousand and two.

This means there are far fewer number words to remember than the twenty-seven in the Greek system, the twenty-eight in the Paiela body counting method, and the many words of concrete counting systems.

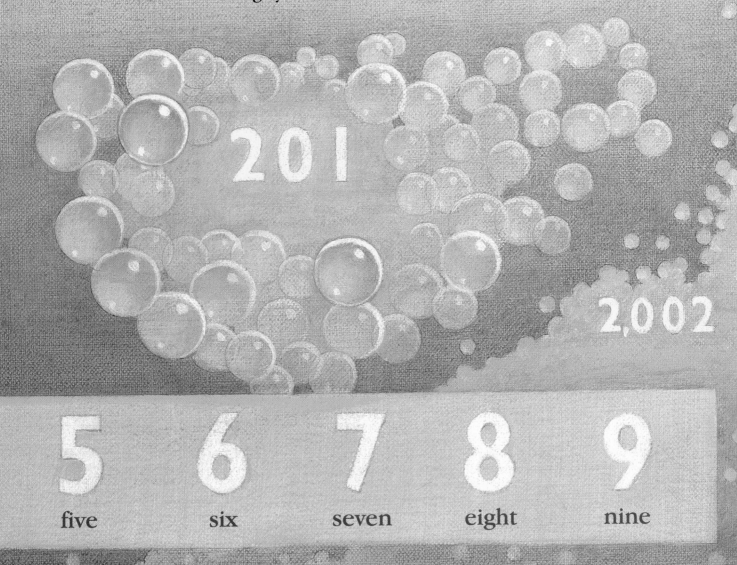

5	6	7	8	9
five	six	seven	eight	nine

The third advantage of Arabic numerals is a better place value system. Unlike previous systems:

- Each digit has a variable, or different, value that depends on where the digit is placed. A four stands for 4, 40, 400, or 4,000, according to whether it is placed in the first, second, third, or fourth position. Its value does not depend on the value of the digit next to it, as in the Roman system, in which XL means forty, but LX is sixty.
- The same ten digits can be used over and over again to count indefinitely. It is not necessary to have different types of signs to indicate units, tens, hundreds, and so on.

The fourth, and greatest, advantage of the Arabic numeral system is the invention of zero. Zero provided a sign for "no unit"—in other words, "none" or "no value." Combined with place value, zero made computing far easier than before because:

- While zero has no value, it shows clearly the place value of each digit of a number. Plus, it marks the place even when there is no unit. For instance, in 1,010, 1 at the far left stands for 1,000; 0 to the right stands for no hundred; 1 to the right stands for 10; and 0 to the far right stands for no unit.

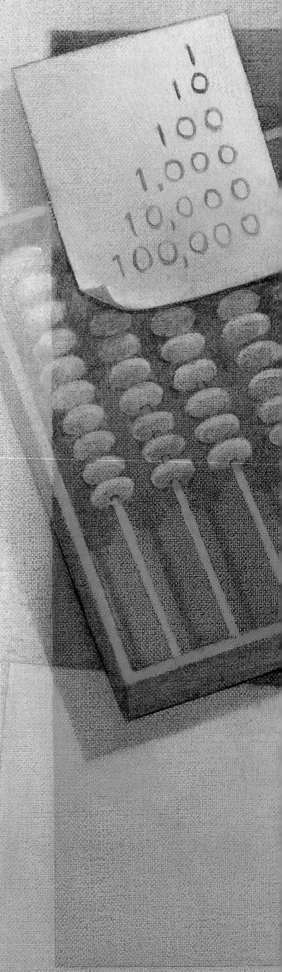

1,010
ONE
THOUSAND
AND TEN

- Zero makes it possible to arrange numerals in columns in order to compute them. In other systems, numerals cannot be arranged this way. Look at this simple addition problem:

$$
\begin{array}{r}
1084 \\
+\ \underline{1797}
\end{array}
$$

To add the Arabic numerals, you line up the numbers in columns, placing the units below the units to the far right, the tens below the tens to the left of the units, the hundreds below the hundreds to the left of the tens, and so on. Then you add the units, note the number of units, carry over the tens, and so on.

Now try to add the corresponding Roman numerals, MLXXXIV + MDCCXCVII. Even if you lined up the units, tens, hundreds, and so on in columns, it wouldn't help.

M		LXXX	IV
M	DCC	XC	VII

- Zero makes it possible to go from unit to ten to hundred, and so on, without changing the shape of signs. Compare 1, 10, 100, and 1,000 with I, X, C, and M.

The invention of Arabic numerals meant a new system of counting and computing!

11:45
ROUTE 94
FIFTH AVE.
NO LEFT TURN 7AM-7PM
SCHOOL DISTRICT 68
12th Annu
BASEBALL SCORES
BEARS 5 JAYS 2
RAMS 4
CUBS 8
LOWER INTEREST
19%
-10
9%
22
19
13
32
33
BOX 970006
63197
60626
7
8
6
4
5
3
2
1

Most of us take our modern system of counting for granted. We forget, or never even realize, that counting had to be invented and that it has been improved upon over a long period of time. In fact, counting was not invented once but many times. This is why various people around the world have different ways of counting, why some societies make more use of numbers than others, and why some systems of counting are more efficient than others.

Counting evolved. In the Middle East, hunters and gatherers counted in a one-to-one relationship around 15,000 B.C.; concrete counting coincided with the beginning of farming around 8000 B.C.; and abstract numbers were invented in the first cities around 3000 B.C.

The invention of abstract numbers was the real starting point of counting. Then bases and place value made the creation of larger and larger numbers possible. Finally, the invention of Arabic numerals with zero made counting limitless and computation simple.

41

GLOSSARY

Abstract counting: when numbers are abstracted, or separated, from the items counted. In other words, when the number words are unrelated to the things counted.

Add: to combine units in a set.

Arabic numerals: the system of numerals used today in the modern world. This system was brought to Europe by the Arabs about A.D. 1000 but was not fully adopted until 1650.

Base: the unit of a number system that is multiplied by itself in order to create a higher number. Some number systems use more than one base.

Body counting: a way of counting used by people who have not developed special number words but count by pointing to parts of their body and, at the same time, saying the corresponding word.

Calculating: computing how many items are in a set.

Computation: the act, method, or result of calculating.

Concrete counting: the use of different sets of numbers to count different categories of things. An example would be the use of different number words to count long things, such as roots; round things, such as oranges; and flat things, such as pancakes.

Concrete number: a numerical expression that combines the ideas of number and thing counted. For example, *twin* combines the ideas of "children of a same birth" and "two."

Counting: to recite numbers in order; to compute how many items there are in a group.

Counting without numbers: matching a set with counters in a one-to-one correspondence.

Decimal system: the system of counting used today in the modern world. It uses base 10, so that a number to the left is

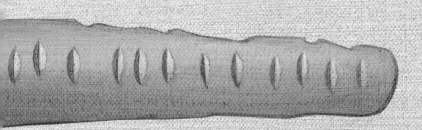

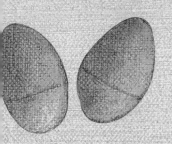

10 times larger than one to the right. Combined with place value and zero, the decimal system allows us to go easily to a different order of magnitude just by moving the place of the digit.

Digits: the first ten numbers, 0 to 9.

Divide: to separate into equal parts.

Equal: of same value.

Googol: a number expressed by a 1 followed by one hundred zeros.

Googolplex: a number expressed by a 1 followed by a googol of zeros.

Hindu numerals: the precursor of Arabic numerals.

Mathematician: a person skilled at the study of numbers.

Mathematics: the study of numbers.

Multiply: to perform a multiplication; to increase a number.

Number: a word expressing how many items there are in a group. Numbers, such as 1, 2, 3, and so on, are part of a set in which they have a fixed order.

Numeral: a sign to write a number.

Place value (also called place notation): when the number takes a different value according to its place. In the decimal system, the same digit has the value of a unit, ten, hundred, thousand, and so on, according to its place in the numeral—for example, 1,111.

Plurality: many; more than one item.

Set: a group of units that belong together.

Subtract: to take away one or more units from a set.

Unit: a precisely specified quantity. In the decimal system, units are the numbers 0 to 9; they are placed to the right of the tens.

Zero: the digit 0, which indicates an absence of a unit.

INDEX

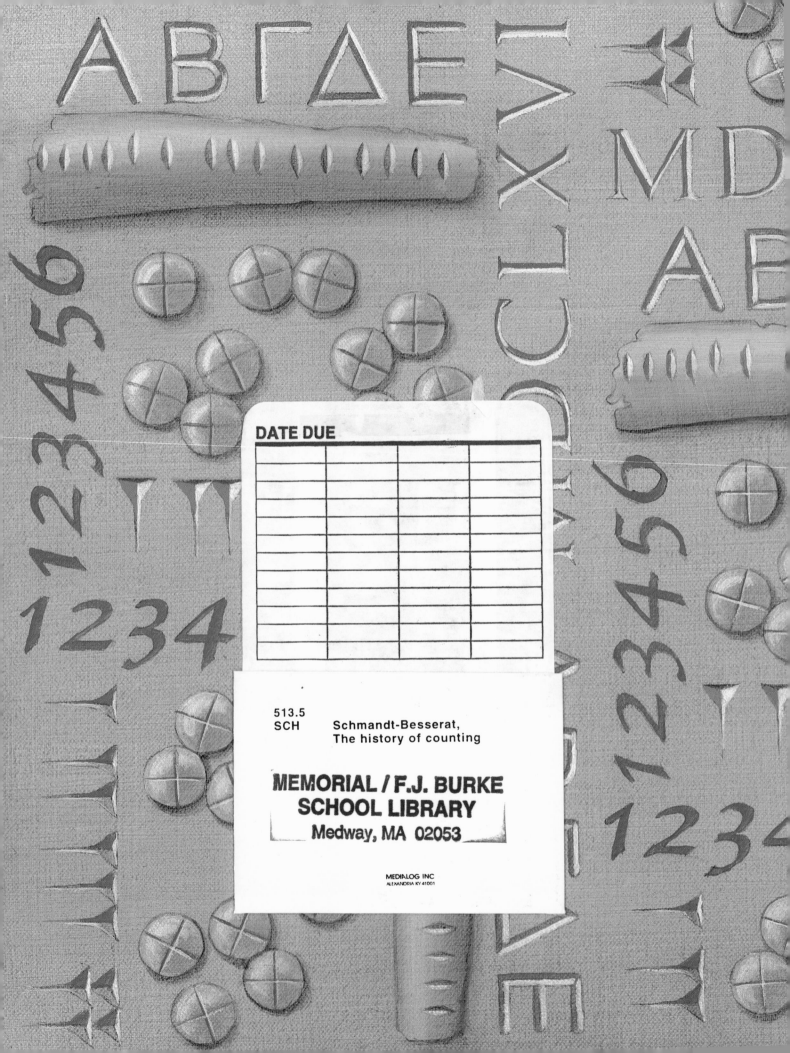